Perfect First Impression -3 Important Seconds

How To Make Unforgettable First Impression In Business, Work Or First Date

by Martin Prodaj

For more visit my web page www.martinprodaj.com

Table of Contents

Copyright

Free Gift

As a way of saying thank you for buying my book, I want to invite you to grab a free check list for perfect first impression. You can grab it here or copy and paste this web address to your browser: http://bit.ly/1zXMh08

Introduction

We aren't living on an abandoned island. If we were, we wouldn't meet many people every day. With many important people, we care about how they look at us. With many important people we care about how we'll impress, the impression we make on them. There have been lots of books and news articles written about first impressions. That could suggest that this topic is particularly interesting or attractive, or even better, really important. Have you ever cared about how people look at you? What they think about you? How they're gonna talk to you? Certainly yes. Every one of us has experienced these kinds of thoughts. Every morning we are confronted with such thoughts to a certain degree. Why else would we stand in front of a closet for long time (women for even longer) thinking what to wear? This morning dilemma shows us that we are trying, consciously or subconsciously, to impress others in a certain way. Simply said, we try to create a good first impression.

There are situations, quite a lot actually, when we shouldn't leave first impressions to chance. For example, an interview for work, business meeting, where we want to convince the customer, or first date; where we want to create a positive image for the other person. In each of these situations, there's only a small window for us to create and leave a perfect first impression. In this couple of seconds, everything is run by the subconsciousness and I don't have enough time or attention for changing or adjusting on the spur of the moment. I have to be ready beforehand. All parts of the puzzle have to fit in with the one and only goal, to create a perfect impression. And that's exactly what this publication will be about.

Perfect Mind Setting

Everything that happens outside happens inside our minds first. Well, this is the most important basic of this book you just learned, so you can lay it aside. Just kidding, stay with me so you're sure that you understood every aspect of this matter. The truth remains though, what others see as a perfect first impression is the reflection of what happens inside our minds. Everything that's happening inside of us is influencing what happens outside of us to a certain degree. It's not rocket science. If we're sad, others see that we're unhappy also. It's the same with all other emotions. Some are harder for the outside world to read than others, but they are all noticeable to the outside watcher.

The question then is, what inside setting should we create that would make the perfect impression for the outside world? What do we need others to notice in the present? And how do we get to it?

CONFIDENCE

Confident people are more successful. They make a better impression. They have better work and earn more money. This claim—and probably another claims—got to you and you started thinking about where these people got this confidence. It probably surprised you that these people don't exceed you significantly in knowledge, work or relationships. Simply put, when you look at them, you see that they are not so different from you. Where, then, is the difference? What's the root of this problem? To understand where confidence is from and how to have enough of it, you have to dig deep down into your memories.

I have a simple exercise for you to find your lost confidence. Try to replay every situation from past when you succeeded in something. It doesn't matter what it was, but the greater success it was the better. Remember the feeling. How was it to experience this success? Awesome, right? How did you feel? Confident? You certainly felt more emotions like, for example, joy, happiness, determination, energy. There's a big probability that you experienced confidence too. That's good news because, basically, you're able to regain this attitude, and right when you're able to do that, you can repeat it.

7

Sometimes people have the feeling like they never were confident and never will be. But that's not true. Everyone certainly achieved something. From every such success confidence is built. The difference is that, in comparison to others, we forget to remind ourselves of this. After some time, this experience is covered with our present lives and we almost never remember those times. We have to fuel our confidence and our achievements are this fuel.

Realise your successes and achievements of your goals as often as possible. Start with a diary of your successes so they become allies, thanks to which you'll have energy for confidence every day. Another idea is to share your successes with other people. But this might seem weird, even awkward to some people. Most of the time when we meet people, we have a tendency to complain about our misfortune, hard times at work and so on. These, though, are no emotions to get confidence from. Exactly the opposite. If you stay for too long in relationships where the negative is brought up, our confidence starts to lower day by day. And that is what you certainly don't need. Share with your friends and aquaintances how you succeeded in something, things you want to say and are proud of.

As time passes, you create a mindset in which positive thought will be present all day. It becomes absolutely natural and you'll never have to regain your confident mindset ever again.

Positive Thinking

Not forcefully. You probably met people in your neighborhood who claim to be the image of positivity. But you can't shake off the feeling that they're not honest. Too much of everything is bad; knowledge from our grandmothers. Extreme positive thinking results in ignoring the reality. But that is not what positive thinking is about. It's actually the opposite.

We can see the reality around us, but even during hard times, we can keep a positive mindset. The basics of generating or creating positive thinking are the same as what we said about building confidence. As with confidence, you search sources of successes and achieved goals; positive thinking is about finding thoughts and emotions of peace, satisfaction and happiness. That's why it's called positive thinking. If you're not positive but want to be, you can consciously start with the process. There are people who are naturally positive, it's part of their personality. If you're unsure of having something like this, you have to do it by yourself. Your goal will be to build positive thinking.

First step is to notice positive things around you. Surround yourself with positive things and positive people. Read books, listen to podcasts, watch TV shows that you know will make you feel good and will bring positive thoughts. Learn to share good and pleasant things with your neighborhood. Surely it wont be easy all the time and you'll find yourself in hard times. It's important not to give up, accept what's happening and keep moving forward.

Perfect Suit

There are situations in life when it's necessary to make a good impression. Career, making new social and business contacts or making a significant deal can depend on it. We'll tell you what to wear so you'll make a good first impression.

APPROPRIATE SUIT FOR JOB INTERVIEW.

Did you get invited for a job interview? Mental preparation is not enough. Although work experience and abilities should be more important, you have to impress with your looks also.

Ladies

Decency should dominate in every lady's outfit chosen for a job interview. A suit with pants or a skirt is ideal. When choosing a skirt, aim for knee length or longer. Definitely not miniskirts, and no big cleavage. If you choose pants, aim for a good length also. In no way should you be dragging them across floor. When it comes to colours, neutrals are the best, like black, grey, brown, blue or a combination of these. Accessories can be part of the outfit as well, but they shouldn't be too big or provocative. The same goes for make-up. Decency has to dominate.

Gentlemen

Men will ruin nothing with a simple but not too social outfit. A shirt is an ideal part. But even in hot seasons it should not have short sleeves. A tie is good but not neccesary, if you do go for a tie, ensure it is the appropriate length. It should be half the length of your belt. If you think that a suit is too flamboyant, elegant pants and a simple sweater are good also. In some branches, formal dressing at the job interview is literally not appropriate. That goes for some art or marketing branches. Because of that, choose your outfit according to the job you are seeking.

WHAT TO WEAR FOR A BUSINESS MEETING.

Some business meetings can be very important for your career. That's why you should dress up so that you'll convince your business partner about your trustworthiness. It's ok to say that outfit for business dealings should look similar to the one for a job interview. A suit for women and men is a classic that won't ruin anything. Focus on the aforementioned details like correct skirt and pants length, decent accessories and a clean, decorated outfit. Men should not forget that the colour of their belt should be the same as the color of their shoes. For women, the colour of their purse should coincide with their shoes. The same goes for colour choosing. Grey, blue, black, white and brown are appropriate for business dealings.

Knowing how to dress up for important opportunities is very important. You also should be dressing up properly for everyday tasks. How to?

5 GENERAL TIPS FOR MEN

It's not a rarity that men have a problem with coordinating items of dress. If there's no advice from women, the result can be horrible. So, dear gentlemen, might it be anywhere, remember these rules.

- White socks don't go well with dark pants and shoes! It's important to accord colour of socks with pants and shoes.
- The next very big mistake is with wearing socks with sandals. These don't belong together at all.
- Pants (especialy elegant) should reach the beginning of the heel. Bunched up pants on shoes don't look good. Same goes for uncovered calves.
- Dirty nor creased dress doesn't belong in public! If you can't iron them yourself and your wife isn't close by, choose another outfit.
- Don't mix apples with pears. Checked shirt with striped pants... Not even by mistake.

Fashion faux pas happen many times when it comes to men, but these are the most common. Maybe fashion will change over time but now... Such combinations are now out!

5 TIPS FOR LADIES

It's a common saying that ladies are more fashion knowledgable, but the differences between genders are smaller everyday, meaning that ladies also aren't always the best in fashion. What should they wear?

- Do you love dresses and skirts? Use your brain when choosing them. Too short is more for teenagers. Pretty legs are visible in longer skirts also!
- Provocative cleavage. Are you proud of your body? Show it, but not in the way that makes you look cheap. Sometimes, less is more.
- Do you know Coco Chanel said that no woman in good shoes can be ugly? Well, it's true. Ruined and worn shoes belong in the trashcan. Even if they're your favourite...
- Always choose accessories, jewellery and bijouterie! They can bring life to your outfit. But take advice from Coco here also. She says that the last accessory that you use should be subtle. Too much is bad.
- Every woman should have something special in her closet. 'Little black dress', quality coat, classic elegant black pants, white blouse and quality jeans. You most certainly will find a good use for them.

It applies also here that outfit should always be clean, ironed and not damaged. But a true lady certainly knows what to wear.

COLOURS ARE IMPORTANT

Do you have a favourite one that you often use in combination? It's good to know that you can say many things with the colour of outfit.

1. Black. Where we live, it's a colour of sadness and that's why we use it for funerals. But black can also be used to convey elegance, especially when combined with white. Women love it because it optically makes them thinner. Those who wear it are taken as unapproachable, or even mysterious, but also serious.

2. White. Colour of cleanness, innocence, even sterility. Same as black, this colour is perfect for combining. Never dress up in a completely white dress! You're gonna make the impression of a doctor or a cook.
3. Yellow. Warm and optimistic colour, but also very bright. Therefore it's better for informal occasions. It should be worn on little parts of the outfit, like accessories.
4. Red. Considered a colour of passion, desire and love. Mostly worn by confident people who want attention. Probably because it's the colour women like on social occasions, but doesn't belong to work.
5. Blue. This is the colour of heaven, worn by peaceful and balanced people. Cold blue can be combined with warmer green. This combination looks fresh and original. Blue is also the universal colour that's appropriate for many occasions and you can't ruin anything with it. If you choose blue for a business meeting, it's a good decision. It'll give the impression of trusthworthiness.
6. Green is the colour of nature and considered as positive and worn by trustworthy people. That's why it's good for business meetings. It's good to combine it with brown.
7. Brown is also warm and peaceful. It's very good to combine and, like black and white, good to wear on a regular day.

As the time passes, gold, bronze and silver is more and more often to be found in closets. These colours are favourites of confident people who like success and luxury. Still, they aren't very good for business dealings or job interviews, but good for ceremonial events.

An outfit says a lot about its wearer, important for first impressions. If it's supposed to be positive, be careful to choose the appropriate outfit for every occasion.

Perfect Verbal Communication

So, you're past the first part of making a first impression through nonverbal communication. It is 55% of our communication and can be considered as the most important factor in creating a first impression. But not the only one. Even if you look good, it will be expected from you to communicate verbally, and this can be decieving. I could write a whole book about this communication, but I'm gonna make it simple and talk about the most important factors that you should focus on so they won't cause trouble.

ACTIVE LISTENING

Active listening is the basic factor of every good conversation. But we're many times, or mostly, coming into contact with active nonlistening. You certainly witnessed such a situation when you said something but had a feeling that the other person wasn't listening or wasn't paying attention to what you said. It's a very common situation and certainly doesn't feel right. How to be an active listener?

It's not as hard as one would assume. You need three factors—paraphrasing, summarisation and using open questions.

PARAPHRASE

Paraphrasing is a process when you try to catch what the other person wants to say and then try to rephrase it using your own words. For example: "If I understand correctly, you had a hell of a day yesterday and, as if that wasn't enough, you got into an argument with your wife." It's important that you're gonna be honest and to the point. The point of paraphrasing is empathy and to understand what the other person is saying.

SUMMARIZATION

Sometimes there is much information and you can get lost in it. As soon as our conversation loses structure, it's hard to orientate in it. Summarisation or simplifying of what was said is a big help, not only for you but also for the other person. If you want to sumarise, you have to pay attention to what has been said and keep it in mind after some while to put it together. Summarisation and paraphrasing is mostly used together.

It's extremely important to summarise during a business meeting or conference. Much information is present, but there's no one to give it structure and order.

If you learn to use summarisation and paraphrasing, you're gonna be a great listener.

FOCUS

Summarisation and paraphrasing is something visible from the outside. Focusing is taking place inside of you. But, if you think about it, summarisation and paraphrasing won't be successful without focusing. What's good focusing about? It's actually very simple. Good focusing is a state of mind when you're focused on one object or activity and doing it for a prolonged period of time. When we notice something else, focusing is gone. The more nervous you are, the harder it is to focus.

It's easy to focus on pleasant things. And that's actually where the secret of good focusing lies. Try to find in someone's conversation something that you find interesting, something that can catch your attention. If there's nothing, try to focus on the pace, voice tone or something else that's interesting for you.

People often ask me if they can't act as if they were interested. I say no, because we can notice quickly that someone isn't listening or not paying attention to what we say. We can uncover it. And so can other people. Sometimes it's quite quick and easy to tell. It's enough if you look at your watch or check your mobile phone and it's clear that you're not interested. Sometimes we ourselves don't realise it untill the other person warns us.

ASKING OPEN QUESTIONS

The third extremely important element is asking questions. Asking questions is the first sign of paying attention. Open questions are creating a place for the next conversation. You are expressing your interest.

Examples of open questions?

> "what do you think about it?"
> "how do you feel about it?"
> "what's your opinion?"
> "how was it for you?"

Of course, after asking an open question you should pay attention to the answer.

The opposite of open questions are closed questions. These are mostly answered with a single sentence or word. For example:

> " what's your name?"
> " where do you live?"
> " what did you eat for dinner today?"

Doesn't sound very pleasing, right? That's why these are also called interrogation questions and should be used as little as possible in conversations—of course, if you're not a detective.

EXPRESSING UNDERSTANDING

We are pleased when others understand us. Aiming for understanding from others is one of our basic motives in communicating. It's very important for us. And these are also motives for others who we want to impress and make a perfect first impression on. Understanding is mostly expressed in these ways:

- aha, I understand
- hmmm
- interesting
- I know how you felt
- I can imagine what it meant to you
- I can understand that

I believe that it's clear that you should mean it honestly from the heart. If you're not empathic, don't attempt to express it. You'll risk that it will seem forced and dishonest and you certainly don't want others to think of you as a forced and dishonest person.

16

USING THE VOCABULARY OF A SECOND PERSON

The vocabulary and sentence structure of every person is like a fingerprint or snapshot of the eye, unique and unrepeatable. It's showing our personality, problems and interests. Identifying this level of communication requires high communication skills. If you're capable of it, you'll reach a completely new quality of mutual understanding.

How do you achieve it? You have to listen very well to what the other person is saying, which words she uses; in internet marketing, we would say what keywords she uses. These keywords are the key to understanding the other person. Uncover them, use them and you'll reach brand new levels of mutual understanding.

Another effective technique is so called "chaining". Chaining in communication means you're using the last words that the other person said, for example, "Well, we didn't manage to go on our vacation," and you answer with, "Hmm, not managing to go on vacation, that must've been unpleasant." There are many factors of active listening present simultaneously—chaining, summarising, paraphrasing and expressing understanding.

The more factors you use in your communication, the better. But be careful so that it won't be unnatural and forced.

Perfect Nonverbal Communication

Perfectly managed nonverbal communication is the key to creating a perfect first impression. Nonverbal communication isn't the only factor but is considered as the most important. It constitutes 55% of all communication signals that we send out to others. If we stood in front of a group of people and didn't say anything, you still would send out certain signals which they could notice and decipher. That's why it's pointless to speak in first 2-3 seconds because people pay more attention to your nonverbal communication.

It's important to realise that nonverbal communication is strongly influenced by our inner feelings, what mood you're in. There was more about it in first chapter. If you're in a positive and confident mindset, your body will reflect this through nonverbal communication. But there are times of unease and during them it's essential to purposely help our body. We can focus on those most important components of nonverbal communication.

We'll go through them one by one.

First, we look at the summarisation of basic elements:

- Mimic: Everything that happens on our face
- Gesticulation: Our hands accompany our verbal expression
- Posturic: Posture of our body
- Kinesics: Body movement
- Proxemics: Proximity to others

And now how to use nonverbal communication to create a perfect first impression.

EYES

Eyes are windows into souls. Quite a poetical comparision. On the other hand, quite practical also because the way people look at us and we look at them and their expression in the eyes says incredibly much. If you didn't see anything but eyes, you could still say quite accurately how someone feels, sad, happy, angry or other strong emotions. It's appropriate to say that the eyes are the first indicators of our feelings.

Expression in our eyes is more than anything else influenced by how we feel and it's quite hard to change that, but we can change, for example, eye contact.

For a great first impression, it's necessary to make and remain eye contact with the other person. With eyes you express your interest. Look at the person in front of you. Notice him. Look her in the eye. But no intimidating staring. It should run across their face and then return. Avoid nervous staring. If you avoid eye contact totally, you create a bad image about yourself. The absence of eye contact can be interpreted as nervousness, insecurity or fear. You don't want to express these.

SMILE

Smiling goes hand in hand with eye contact. Face is right after eyes in importance in how people can see how you feel. It's important to smile, but not a forceful smile, an honest smile that comes from your soul. If that's not possible, you could act it out. Fake it till you make it. Studies have shown that an acted smile can affect us and turn into an honest smile.

It can sometimes look unnatural or forced, but try one exercise. It's especially useful if you feel bad. Stand in front of a mirror and smile at yourself. You might feel stupid, but keep at it. Smile at yourself, you can also make some grimaces, but notice how it affects you. If studies are right, you should feel better. Try and see.

BODYPOSTURE

The problem with nonverbal communication is about us not realising it. It's subconscious. In most cases, it's good because we don't have to control our standing, walking or expressing, but sometimes this autopilot isn't best and we need to regain control. Body posture and its meaning can be interpreted from far away. It's from ancient times when people had to decide whether the other person was a threat or not from far away. This isn't needed so much in present times, but the identification mechanism stayed. It means that we are quite easily readable to others. Our posture gives it out. There are couple of signals that we should learn to control:

- Straight back, chest popping out. Position that's by itself confident. If accompanied by a confident look in the eyes, a perfect impression is in our pockets.
- Open hands. In ancient times a sign that we don't hold any weapon and therefore aren't dangerous. Today it's more of a sign that we don't hide anything.
- Slightly straddled legs. This stance gives us stability and stability gives us confidence. Confidence, again, gives a perfect first impression.
- Tilted body. If you sit and want to express interest, slightly tilt your body towards the person. Generally we have the tendency to tilt towards things we are interested in or find attractive. Recall those love birds you saw. How they tilt towards each other. The opposite is tilting back, which we do when we don't like something. Imagine a smelly food, certainly you would tilt back.
- Don't forget to smile.

HANDSHAKE

First contact impression you get with the other person. Until now it was all about looking. Touch is much more personal. A handshake was also a sign of us not holding any weapon and not being dangerous. Generally we know two types of handshake. First, absolutely inappropriate and unfortunate is the so called dead fish. Maybe you experienced it; someone walks to you during a conference or in a discussion for a handshake and offers a hand without any tension, energy and strength. Ideally, a handshake should be short, energetic and strong. With the first handshake, we express who we are, that we are strong and confident.

Another extreme is crushing bones, mostly done by strong men who want to express their dominance. From the social perspective, also an unfortunate situation and should be avoided. Such handshake can truly be painful for the other person and certainly won't create a positive impression. What should a correct handshake look like? Short, energetic and strong (not too much), maybe accompanied by a short shake.

In an official setting we try to avoid touching with the other hand, a dangerous situation where you need a first impression.

With control, you have all the elements of a flawless first impression, everything should be running automatically and subconsciously. Aquiring of a flawless first impression is a matter of time. If you're not good at it, the first noticable results could be expected after a month or two of intense training, during which you work with your inner setting and nonverbal communication, just like with other factors of a perfect first impression. But let's take a detailed look at some common situations where a first impression is extremely important. It's possible to say that your future will be based on your first impression.

Job Interview

We probably wouldn't find any other sphere where the importance of a first impression is taking place more often than during interviews for jobs. No wonder. Your potential employee wants only the best. That's why personalists are trained for uncovering and deciphering the person in front of them. The impression on people around you is one of those they focus on. Let's go through the individual steps of a job interview and what's important to do.

PREPARATION

Despite the fact that being prepared for a job interview should be a certainty, personalists are often saying to us that candidates aren't prepared. What does it mean?

- They don't know, or at least aren't sure what position are they interested in. Many people are just blindly sending their resumes hoping that someone notices them. That's a waste of time with a slight possibility of success. The same goes for a businessman who tries to sell everything to everyone. Such a business man, in the end, won't sell anything. Don't be like a careless seller who doesn't care who, where, how and and to whom he sells something.
- They don't know anything about the company they wanna work with.
- They don't know and can't say how the company would benefit from their work.
- They think of them too highly. It's important to be confident, but if your confidence isn't backed up with relevant and provable evidence, it's a house of cards. A couple of seconds are enough to crash your intensely built image just like a house of cards.

WELCOMING AND SELF-PRESENTATION

From the moment you meet your interviewer, you have 3 seconds. During these 3 seconds an image about you is being created. This is why you should be fully aware of these 3 seconds. During these 3 seconds, you should be in control of everything. You can later leave it to subconsciousness, but for now, focus. What should you focus on?

- You're waiting to enter an office or meeting room. Leave nothing to coincidence. Watch out. Close before being invited, stand up so that you won't stand up after they invite you because you will lose time, attention and you could damage something while standing up.
- From the moment the personalist shows up, keep eye contact and smile.
- Reach out with your hand, grab the offered hand and say your name together with greeting clearly.
- When you enter the room, wait untill they tell you to sit. If possible, sit more on the edge so that you won't sit face to face. It's considered as confronting and you want to avoid that.
- If they offer something to drink, choose water. A good reason for that is when you spill it, it won't be too much of a problem to remove it, unlike tea or coffee.
- If you're stressed, try to breathe in and out deeply a couple of times. Some experts say that you should openly confess it as it should make you seem more human and authentic. Personally, I like this advice, why hide something obvious? I'd rather confess that I'm nervous than risk being caught.
- Self-presentation. Part of many job interviews is some form of self-presentation. Simply put, it could be understood as a short mini presentation in front of audience, mostly on a given topic and to introduce yourself. It's about showing your presentation skills. It's good to prepare yourself at home. It should be brief, dynamic and interesting. It should immerse listeners and ideally contain a funny story. During this you should keep eye contact and have loosened nonverbal expression. It's essential to include interactive elements like questions for the audience or rhetorical questions. There's a lot to say about presentation so a little bit of research comes in handy.
- Try to be loosened and natural the whole time. Keep eye contact and smile. If you manage to get at least some of it, your chances of success will increase.

Business Meeting

Under business meeting we'll mean a meeting that we organise with the purpose of agreeing on business cooperation. It's mostly a situation when you're trying to sell your product or service to a potential buyer, exchange a couple of emails, inform each other about what you're offering and what the other person wants and needs, and now it's time for a personal meeting which is important for future cooperation. Let's take a look at it.

PREPARATION

If you're not new in business then you certainly know that preparing yourself for the meeting is a basic condition for succeeding. Maybe you're gonna read what you know but repetition can't hurt.

- Summarise all information in one place. Evernote is good for keeping emails, websites and personal notices together. The point is to have them in a place that you can access quickly and know where to search. It's not pleasant not to be able to find required data when you need them. The built up stress won't help your impression.
- Pay extreme caution to your outfit. We already spoke about it. Everything must be perfect. Your suit, shirt, tie, shoes have to meet the most strict quality requirements. Don't underestimate this step, it could cost you a great business opportunity.
- I don't want to go too deep into business, there's another publication for that, but there's one basic rule where many businessmen fail. Before you start to offer anything, listen and then present your offer.
- In a company that invited you, you're a guest, behave like it. Being confident is good; being cocky is bad. Not good for a good impression.
- Although it might not primarily belong to creating a first impression, it's often advised to notice everything around you where you've been invited. Every office is a reflection of its owner. Noticing surroundings can help you find out more about the person than you would from talking to him. What you see can be used. Did you notice some sport trophies? Does it look like the company owner is a passionate athlete, or even a

successful one? This topic can be used in a conversation. If you're also interested in that particular sport, your chances of succeeding increase rapidly.

- For greetings the same applies that we said about the job interview. What's particulary important is where you position yourself. If possible, avoid deep and soft chairs in which you'll literally lose your ground. Choose a classical conference chair.

10 Tips on How to Make a Perfect Impression on a First Date

Realise that the impression you make after a first date might influence your life. Maybe you're going on a date with your future lifelong partner. We'll give you tips on how to make a good impression. If you combine them, you won't ruin anything.

1. Take caution on dressing up. Especially based on where the date is going to take place. If it's going to be a luxurious restaurant or a theatre, dress up elegantly. If you're going on a romantic walk or a picnic in a park, adjust your dress accordingly.

2. Be clean and well conditioned. Let it be anything, make sure your dress being clean, ironed and not ruined! The same goes for shoes. Outfit and footwear in a bad condition isn't appropriate to wear anywhere, especially to a first date.

3. Choose appropriate colours. Red and purple are colours of love and passion. In particular, ladies won't ruin anything on a first date with these colours. Avoid black and dark grey.

4. Be yourself. Ladies, if you don't like a skirt, don't choose it on a date either. Realising that a skirt is for only an occasional choice for you could lead to disappointing your partner. The same goes for gentlemen and suits. If you wear a suit on a first date and then show up in torn jeans, she won't be very happy. Simply be yourself.

5. Smile. Is it repetitive? You probably won't be willing to meet a grumpy and negative person again. Smiling and positive people leave a good impression. But of course, too much of everything is bad. Avoid infantile laugh after every sentence with your partner. You don't want to look like teenager lovebirds!

6. Hands will reveal a lot. If you don't want to look unconditioned, your nails should be taken care of and kept clean. Ladies should not have worn off nail polish. Everyone is stressed on a first date and doesn't know what to do with their hands. Try to not scratch your head, touch your face too much or even worse, don't light up one cigarette after another. Especially on a date with a non-smoker.

7. Don't overdo it with sex appeal! This goes more for ladies. You don't want to look vulgar or cheap. Are you looking for a lifelong partner or a couple of nights? See-through tops and short skirts should be a taboo.

8. Take caution with makeup and jewellery! If you want to grab a partner's attention, don't put on a mask of makeup. You'll seem unnatural. And you certainly don't want your partner to not be able to recognise you after a morning coffee. Same goes for jewellery – less is sometimes more.

9. Relax. Your outfit will certainly help you to feel better. Try to be peaceful and relaxed. Your life is not at stake! The best thing for you is to be yourself. Drink a glass of wine if you can't relax. But definitely don't get drunk.

10. Have an intelligent conversation. Even if dressed up flawlessly with a perfect look, cockiness, swearing and monologues exclusively about yourself will certainly ruin a good impression. Realise that you're both on a date. Listen to the other person and try to find out about her as much as you can. If you can't find any common interests and there's nothing to discuss, it's like you haven't found your soul mate. But chin up! Continue searching...

It's quite easy. A smile, appropriate outfit and intelligent conversation will assure success. The rest is up to you two.

Conclusion

Do you know where the real secret of a perfect impression lies? In you knowing what you have to do. And you, based on this guide, should be capable of that. But that's not all. You have to review all of your actions. You have to watch your surroundings, people's reactions and, based on that, know whether you're improving or not. It's important to know that it's about constant self-improvement of your performance and looks. But the most important is creating quality relationships where you'll be yourself, and, in doing that, as always, I wish you the best.

About Author

PaedDr.Martin Prodaj. Lecturer, coach, speaker, published author. Ha has been working on many HR positions in big companies as Amslico AIG, ING, Slovak Telekom, Telefonica O2, Thyssen Krupp, Eden Red and many others. He has been working with individuals as well. He has many experiences with almost every HR tool, like AC, DC, talent management, design and realization of soft skills trainings (presentation skills, sale skills, managerial skills, running different kind of workshops and seminars). He published book Work Life Balance. He is also blogger, video blogger, author of many info products and video online courses. He published more than 200 videos on his youtube channel martoprody

He is living in Slovakia, Bratislava.

You can find more information on his web page www.martinprodaj.com.

Connect With Me

Web page: www.martinprodaj.com

Twitter: @martinprodaj

Connect with me on LinkedIn: linkedin.com/in/martinprodaj

Facebook: https://www.facebook.com/Martin-Prodaj-CoachingConsulting

Other Books by Martin Prodaj

- <u>Human Resources Development: 10 principles How to Achieve the Best From Your Employees for Human Resources,</u>

Last but not least

I must thank you for deciding to purchase my book. I am sure that you had many other options to choose from, but you decide for me. And for this I am very grateful.

I would like ask you for favor. Could you please take a few moments of your time, to leave your review for this book an Amazon?

Just a couple of words...your simple thoughts about this book will allow me to improve the quality of my other books.

Thank you very much.

I wish you the best of luck in your life and business.

If you have any questions, comments, suggestions, or ideas about this ebook, please let me know.

If you find any mistakes or typos PLEASE tell me by sending the error and page you found it on to my email

martin.prodaj@gmail.com

Feel free to email me if you need any help to get things done.

www.ingramcontent.com/pod-product-compliance
Lightning Source LLC
Chambersburg PA
CBHW020959180526
45163CB00006B/2424